Treasures From the Attic

Exploring Fractions

M. Katherine Gavin, *University of Connecticut*

Linda Jensen Sheffield, *Northern Kentucky University*

Judith Dailey, *Connecticut Association for Mathematically Precocious Youth*

Suzanne H. Chapin, *Boston University*

Student Mathematician's Journal

Common Core State Standards

Kendall Hunt
publishing company

www.kendallhunt.com
Send all inquiries to:
4050 Westmark Drive
Dubuque, IA 52002
1-800-542-6657

The contents of this book were developed in part with funding from a grant from the Department of Education, Jacob K. Javits Gifted and Talented Students Education Act. However, these contents do not necessarily represent the policy of the Department of Education, and you should not assume endorsement by the Federal Government.

ISBN 978-1-4652-6221-9

Printed in the United States of America

1 2 3 4 5 6 7 8 9 10

Production Date: 2016
Printed by: LSI, LaVergne TN

United States of America
Batch number: 436221

TABLE OF CONTENTS

Chapter 1: Making Sense of Fractions

Lesson 1: Measure Treasures

Lesson 2: Frolicking Frogs

Lesson 3: Peppermint Stick Candy Counter

Lesson 4: Daddy Long Legs Wins at the Fair!

Chapter 2: Making Sense of Operations with Fractions

Lesson 1: Sew What

iv

CLASSROOM DISCUSSIONS

You have the right to ask questions.

You have the right to make a contribution to an attentive, responsive audience.

You have the right to be treated respectfully.

You have the right to have your ideas discussed, not you.

Rights

You are obligated to speak loudly enough for others to hear.

You are obligated to listen to others in order to understand.

You are obligated to agree or disagree with the speaker's comments and explain why.

Obligations

Adapted from Chapin, S.H., O'Connor, C., & Anderson, N. C. (2013). *Classroom discussions using math talk to help students learn, grades K–6* (3rd ed.). Sausalito, CA: Math Solutions Publications.

THINKING LIKE A MATHEMATICIAN*

Here is a list of skills mathematicians use every day. See how many you can use in your Student Mathematician's Journal.

1. Make sense of problems and keep trying until you solve them.

2. Understand quantities, their relationships, and how to represent them.

3. Build logical reasons to defend your thinking. Consider the reasoning of others and ask useful questions to help make sense of the reasoning. Explain why you agree or disagree with another's reasoning.

4. Use the math you know to help solve problems in everyday life. Use physical models, drawings, tables, graphs, and/or equations to help you.

5. Choose and use the appropriate math tools to help solve each problem.

6. Communicate explanations clearly using correct math vocabulary and symbols.

7. Look closely and use patterns to help solve problems.

8. Notice if you are using the same math again and again and look for short cuts.

9. Solve a problem in a new way. Ask new questions to investigate.**

---

* Adapted from the Common Core State Standards: Standards for Mathematical Practice

National Governors Association Center for Best Practices (NGA Center), Council of Chief State School Officers (CCSSO). (2010). *Common Core State Standards for Mathematics.* Washington, DC: Retrieved from http://www.corestandards.org/the-standards.

** Johnsen, S. K., & Sheffield, L. J. (Eds.). (2013). *Using the common core state standards for mathematics with gifted and advanced learners.* Waco, TX : Prufrock Press.

Project M³: Treasures From the Attic

MATHEMATICIANS WRITE ON!

When you write in your Mathematician's Journal:

1. Read the questions. Make sure you understand every part and vocabulary word in the questions.

2. Brainstorm ideas.

3. Write your answer.

4. Read over your answers and check that you:

   a. answered all of the questions;
   b. defended your answers by using vocabulary words, drawings, numbers, and/or other details.

5. Revise your answers if you think someone else reading it would not know what you were thinking by asking yourself the following questions:

   a. "Is this clear?"
   b. "Will the reader understand why I did what I did?"

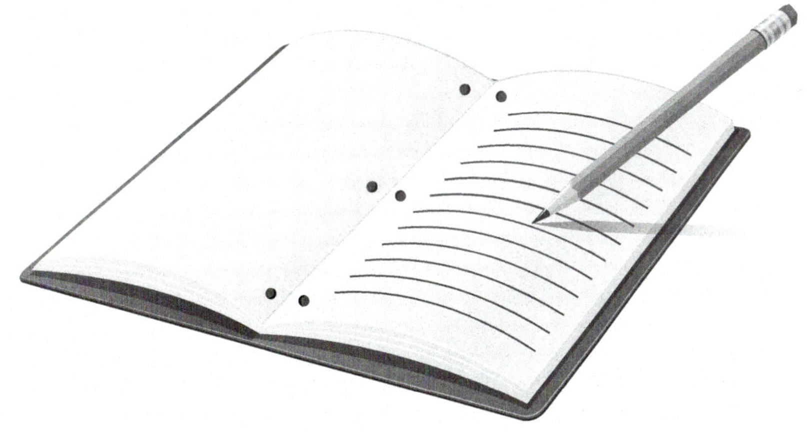

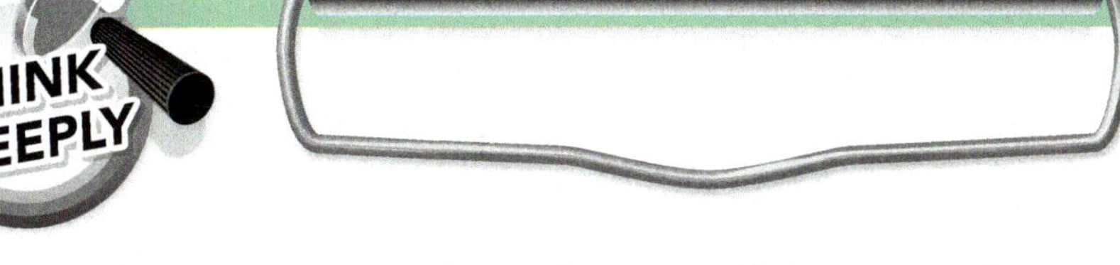

1. What are equivalent fractions? Use numbers, pictures, and words to explain. Do not use $\frac{1}{2}$ as one of your fractions.

MY THOUGHTS AND QUESTIONS

MY RESPONSE

Need more room? Use the next page.

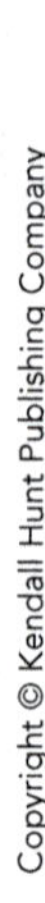

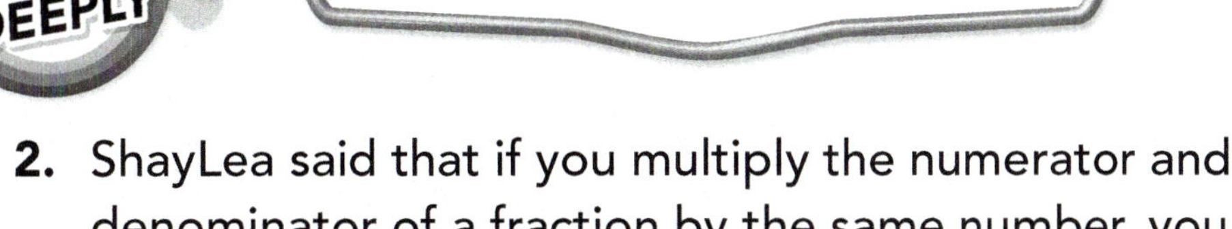

2. ShayLea said that if you multiply the numerator and denominator of a fraction by the same number, you get an equivalent fraction. Is this true? Why or why not?

MY THOUGHTS AND QUESTIONS

MY RESPONSE

Need more room? Use the next page.

Student Mathematician: _______________________________   Date: _______________

Frolicking Frogs

For each of the following, mark an adding machine tape with
the name of the frog and the fractions to indicate how far that
frog jumped. Use a separate adding machine tape for each frog.

Big Green Monster and Swamp Prince

Mark the adding machine tape at $\frac{7}{9}$ foot, the Big Green Monster's first leap of the day at
the Frolicking Frog Jumping Contest at the Washington County Fair. The Swamp Prince
jumped $\frac{5}{6}$ foot for his first leap. Mark a separate adding machine tape to show where the
Swamp Prince landed. Who had the longer jump?

____

____

Lily Pad Lily

Lily Pad Lily first landed at $1\frac{3}{8}$ feet. Mark her first jump on an adding machine tape.
After her second leap, Lily Pad Lily landed on the 2-foot mark. Mark this on the same
tape. Which jump was longer? Explain.

____

____

Magnificent Mike and Marvelous Maxine

Magnificent Mike and Marvelous Maxine were twin leapers from way back. Magnificent
Mike's first leap was $2\frac{2}{3}$ feet, and Marvelous Maxine landed at $\frac{11}{4}$ feet on her first jump.
Mark one adding machine tape to show where Magnificent Mike landed and another to
show where Marvelous Maxine landed. Who jumped farther?

____

____

Bouncing Beauty

Bouncing Beauty's first leap was $\frac{25}{12}$ feet. Mark an adding machine tape to show where she
landed at the end of the jump.

Frisky Frog Leaps

1. Beulah Bubbles landed at $1\frac{2}{3}$ feet on her first jump. Mark additional fractions on the line below to show where Beulah Bubbles landed.

0 $\dfrac{5}{9}$

2. Leaping Lizzie landed at $2\frac{3}{4}$ feet but jumped backwards and landed at $2\frac{5}{8}$ feet. Show where Leaping Lizzie landed on her two leaps below.

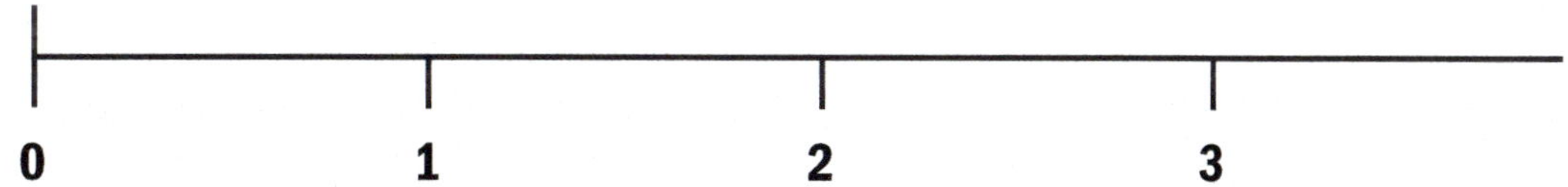

0   **1**   **2**   **3**

3. Create a Frisky Frog Leap situation for a friend to mark on the number line below. Write the answer on the back of this page to compare with what your friend marks.

0   **4**

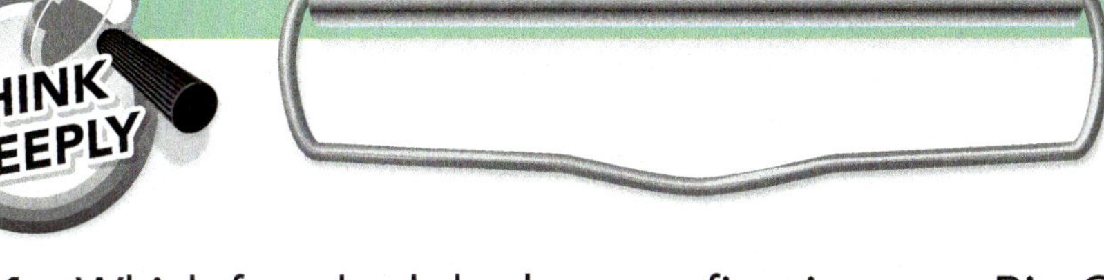

1. Which frog had the longest first jump — Big Green Monster, Swamp Prince, Lily Pad Lily, Magnificent Mike, Marvelous Maxine, or Bouncing Beauty?
Explain your answer.

MY THOUGHTS AND QUESTIONS

MY RESPONSE

Need more room? Use the next page.

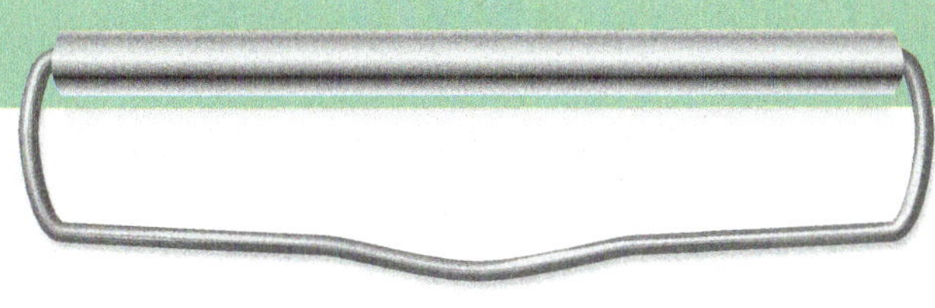

2. Daddy Long Legs had three practice jumps at the fair. His jump of $1\frac{1}{3}$ feet is marked on the number line below. Locate and label his other two jumps of $\frac{5}{12}$ foot and $1\frac{3}{4}$ feet on the number line. Explain your answers.

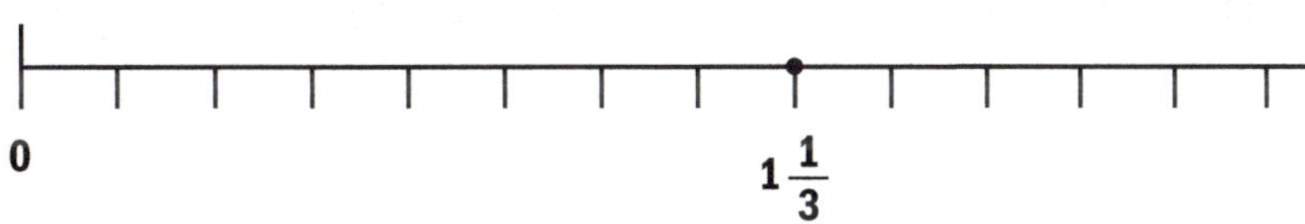

MY RESPONSE

Need more room? Use the next page.

Candy Bag Capers

1. These are less than $\frac{1}{2}$ pound.

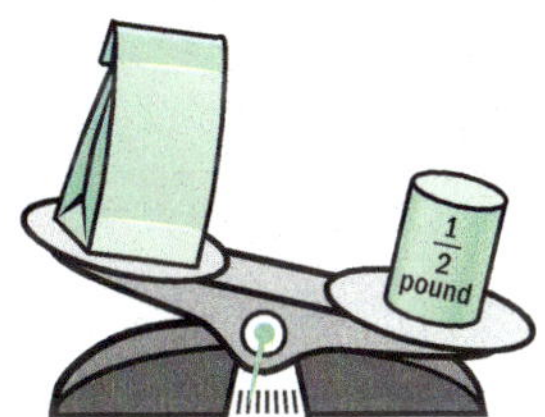

Weight(s)

____

Reason

____

____

2. These are greater than $\frac{1}{2}$ pound but less than 1 pound.

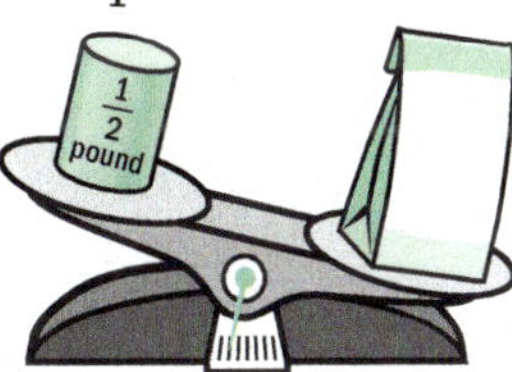

Weight(s)

____

Reason

____

____

3. These are equal to $\frac{1}{2}$ pound.

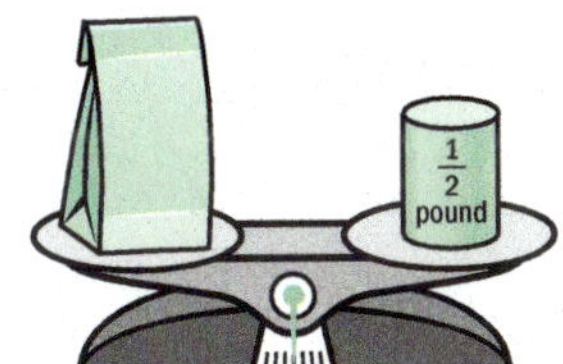

Weight(s)

____

Reason

____

____

4. These are greater than 1 pound but less than $1\frac{1}{2}$ pound.

Weight(s)

____

Reason

____

____

5. List the bags in order from the lightest to the heaviest. _______________________________

____

1. Great-great-grandpa Milotz packaged three bags of chocolate drops. They weighed $\frac{11}{16}$ of a pound, $\frac{5}{8}$ of a pound and $\frac{11}{24}$ of a pound each. Your job is to line the candy bags up on the counter from the least to the greatest. Use at least two different strategies to order them, and explain each strategy.

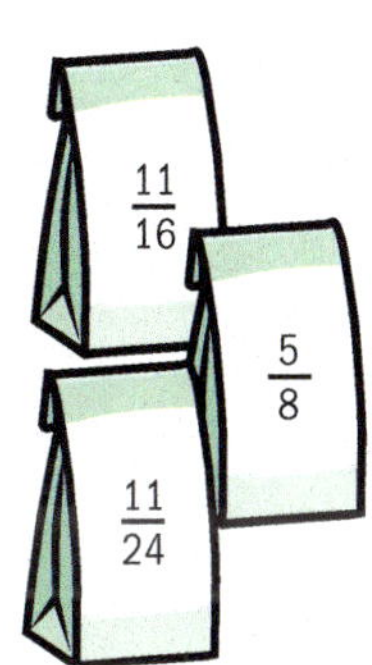

MY THOUGHTS AND QUESTIONS

MY RESPONSE

Need more room? Use the next page.

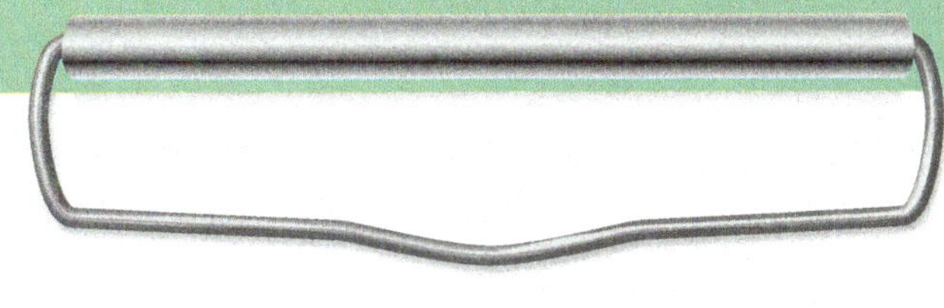

2. Which fraction is larger, $\frac{23}{28}$ or $\frac{3}{4}$? Show how you would use a common denominator to explain your answer.

MY THOUGHTS AND QUESTIONS

MY RESPONSE

Need more room? Use the next page.

Student Mathematician: _________________________________   **Date:** ______________

Proof Page for Daddy Long Legs Story

The editor of *The Javits Gazette* used a grid to help lay out the news stories in the Gazette. The following are different grids that she has used.

A. 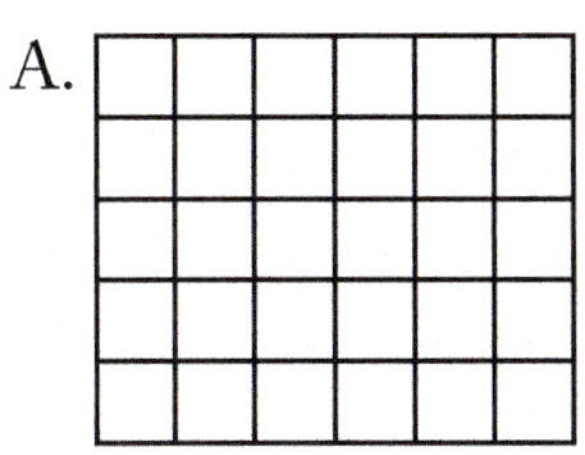   B. 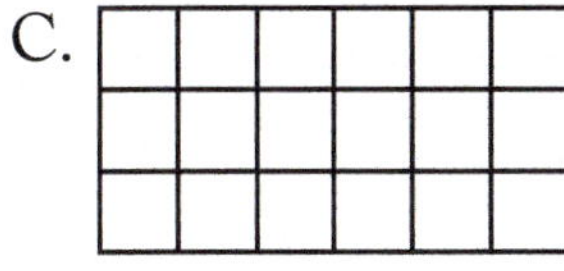   C.

Total squares on page A: ____

Total squares on page B: ____

Total squares on page C: ____

Help the editor design layouts for the pages by dividing each page equally among three stories: Headline 1, Headline 2 and Headline 3. She wants you to make sure that each of the three stories on each page (pages A, B and C) takes up the same amount of space on that page, but the shapes of the stories must be different. That is, the stories should each take up exactly $\frac{1}{3}$ of the space on each page.

Practice Proof Pages for Daddy Long Legs Story

A. 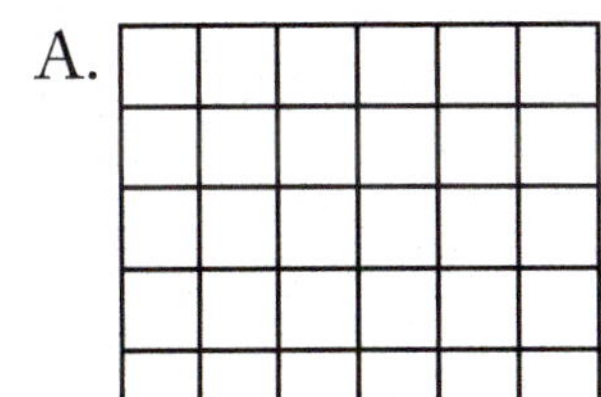   B.    C. 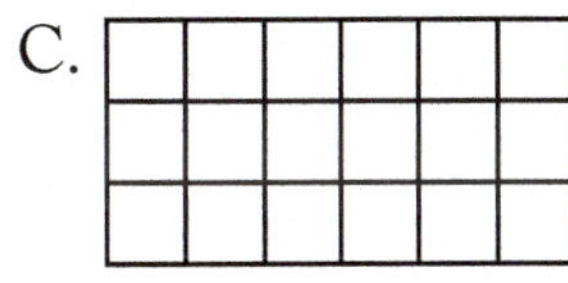

A. 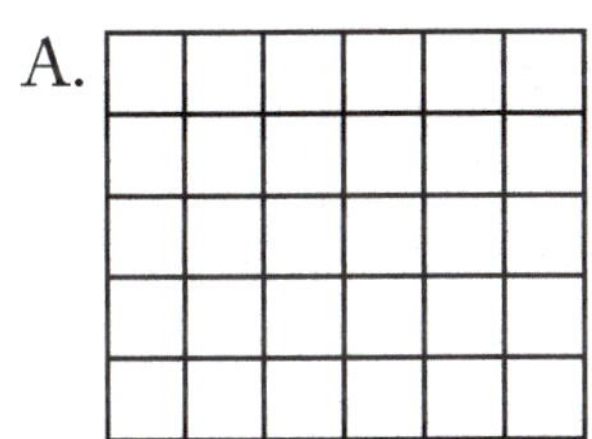   B.    C. 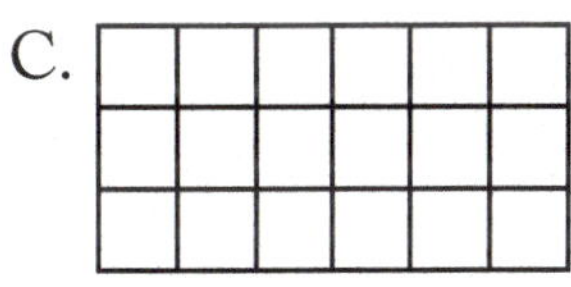

A. 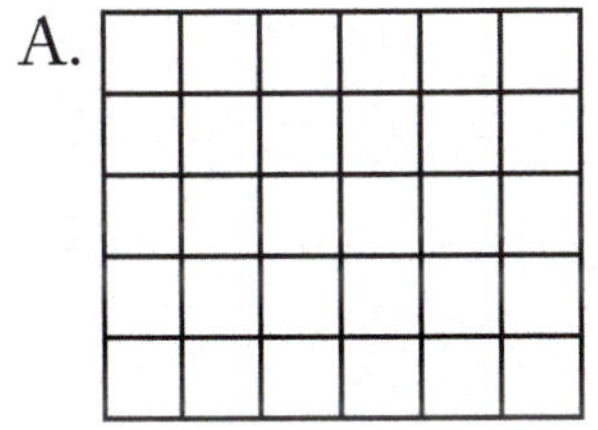   B. 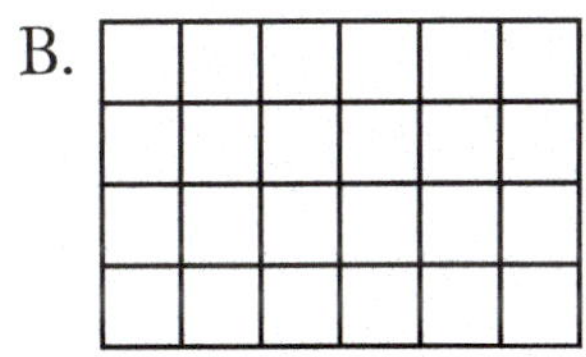   C. 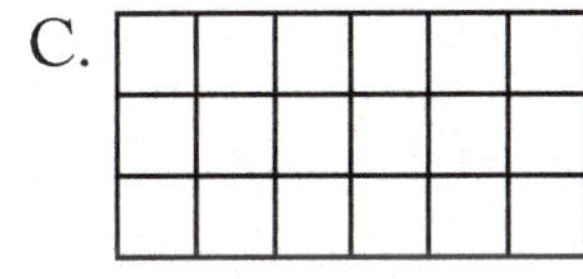

A.   B. 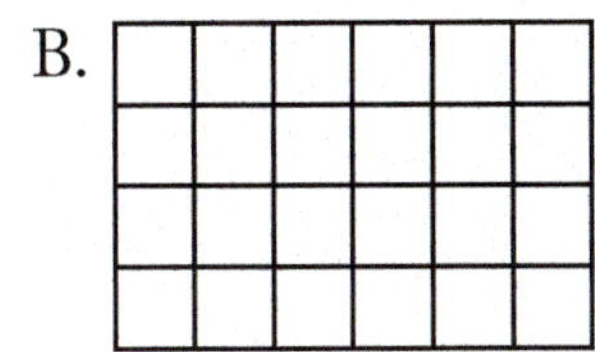   C.

News Items for Proof Copy

The article about Daddy Long Legs filled more of
the front page than any other story. There was also a
picture of Henry Milotz with Daddy Long Legs and
the first place trophy. The other news items reported
on the front page that day were:

- Continued coverage about the pending vote on
  the Nineteenth Amendment ($\frac{1}{4}$ of the page);

- A protest article about Jim Thorpe's Olympic medals being taken away
  from him ($\frac{1}{9}$ of the page);

- A story about the World Peace Treaty that had been signed ($\frac{2}{9}$ of the page);

- And a story about the return of Haliday Smoot from a trip abroad
  ($\frac{1}{12}$ of the page).

1. What part of the front page was devoted to the story and pictures of
   Daddy Long Legs?

   ____

2. What amount of space is taken up by all articles on the front page?
   Show your answer in fractional form and as a whole number.

   ____

3. Create a front page for *The Javits Gazette* and draw a sketch of it on the
   blank paper provided. Include grid lines on your copy to indicate the space
   taken up by each article. Show that you have found the correct amount of
   space for all the articles in the story.

The Javits Gazette News Release

Daddy Long Legs Wins at the Fair!

Henry Milotz's frog Daddy Long Legs won first place at the Washington County Fair. After having very disappointing practice jumps, Daddy Long Legs made three spectacular leaps into the hall of fame. His jumps were $6\frac{3}{4}$ feet, $6\frac{4}{6}$ feet and $6\frac{3}{12}$ feet.

His next closest competitors were Slimy with jumps of $\frac{19}{3}$ feet, $\frac{37}{6}$ feet and $\frac{17}{3}$ feet, and Boggy Meadows with jumps of $5\frac{1}{3}$ feet, $6\frac{3}{4}$ feet and $4\frac{12}{8}$ feet.

Determine which frog had the longest leap and the shortest leap of the contest.

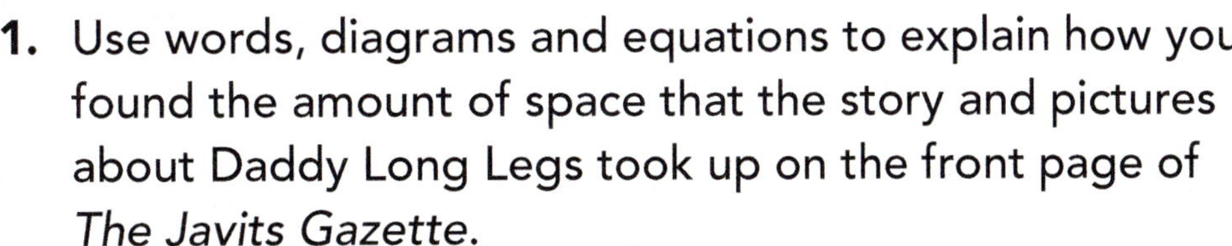

1. Use words, diagrams and equations to explain how you found the amount of space that the story and pictures about Daddy Long Legs took up on the front page of *The Javits Gazette*.

MY THOUGHTS AND QUESTIONS

MY RESPONSE

Need more room? Use the next page.

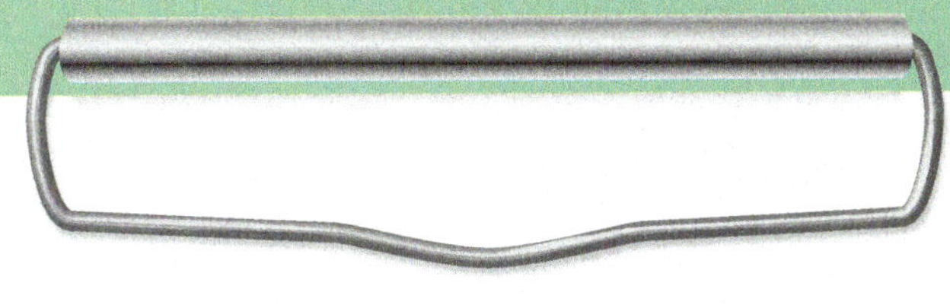

2. Read *The Javits Gazette* news release on Daddy Long Legs. Determine the winners of the longest jump and the shortest jump. Explain your reasoning.

MY THOUGHTS AND QUESTIONS

MY RESPONSE

Need more room? Use the next page.

Is This 1?

For each of the following amounts, determine if the total is less than, equal to or greater than 1. Explain your reasoning.

	Less than 1	Equal to 1	Greater than 1
$\frac{2}{3} + \frac{1}{2}$ Explain:			
$\frac{3}{4} + \frac{1}{3}$ Explain:			
$\frac{5}{8} + \frac{1}{4}$ Explain:			
$\frac{1}{3} + \frac{1}{2} + \frac{1}{4}$ Explain:			
$\frac{2}{8} + \frac{1}{2} + \frac{1}{4}$ Explain:			

Make 1

1. Mrs. Milotz had the following remnants of cloth. Mr. Diwoky needs to buy exactly 1 yard of cloth. List all the different ways that he might buy exactly 1 yard using two remnants.

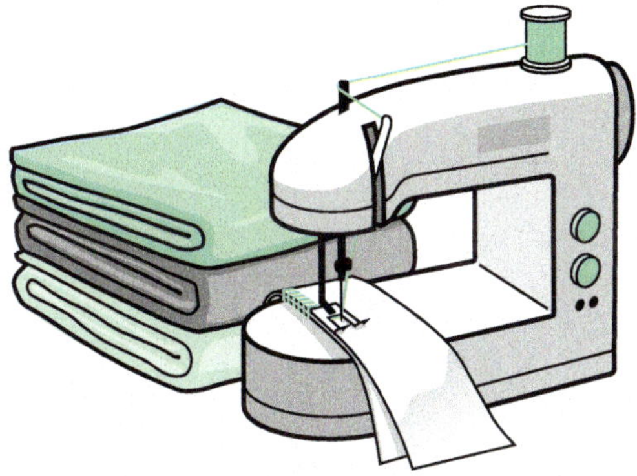

- $\frac{1}{8}$ yard (four pieces available)
- $\frac{1}{6}$ yard (three pieces available
- $\frac{1}{4}$ yard (two pieces available)
- $\frac{1}{3}$ yard (two pieces available)
- $\frac{3}{8}$ yard (two pieces available)
- $\frac{1}{2}$ yard (two pieces available)
- $\frac{5}{8}$ yard (one piece available)
- $\frac{2}{3}$ yard (one piece available)
- $\frac{3}{4}$ yard (one piece available)
- $\frac{5}{6}$ yard (one piece available)
- $\frac{7}{8}$ yard (one piece available)

2. List three other ways that Mr. Diwoky might have purchased exactly 1 yard of cloth if he bought three or more pieces. Use diagrams or equations to show that your choices total exactly 1 yard. You may reuse the remnants with each combination. For example, Mr. Diwoky used $\frac{1}{2}$ twice to make 1 whole when he considered only two remnants. He can reuse those for other combinations.

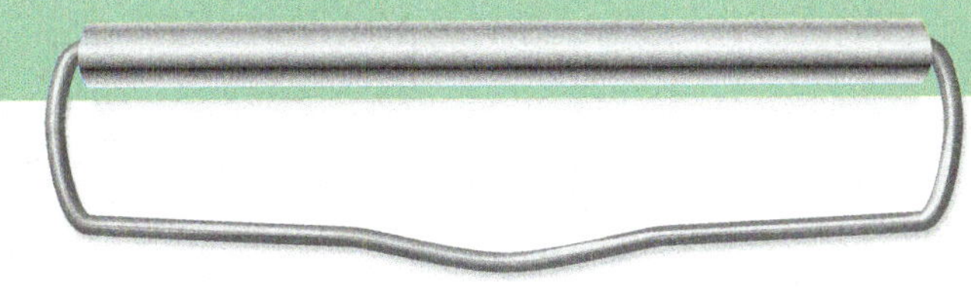

1. Mrs. Milotz has the following remnants of cloth. Mr. Diwoky needs to buy exactly 1 yard of cloth. List at least five different ways that he might buy exactly 1 yard using more than two remnants. (You may reuse the remnants for each combination.)

- $\frac{1}{8}$ yard (four pieces available)
- $\frac{1}{6}$ yard (three pieces available)
- $\frac{1}{4}$ yard (two pieces available)
- $\frac{1}{3}$ yard (two pieces available)
- $\frac{3}{8}$ yard (two pieces available)
- $\frac{1}{2}$ yard (two pieces available)

- $\frac{5}{8}$ yard (one piece available)
- $\frac{2}{3}$ yard (one piece available)
- $\frac{3}{4}$ yard (one piece available)
- $\frac{5}{6}$ yard (one piece available)
- $\frac{7}{8}$ yard (one piece available)

MY THOUGHTS AND QUESTIONS

Need more room? Use the next page.

MY RESPONSE

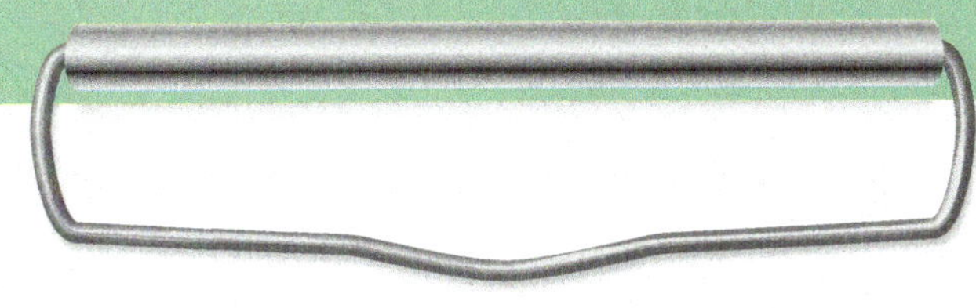

2. J.C. said that he found another way to make a whole, using three pieces, that was not on the list. J.C. says that $\frac{2}{3} + \frac{1}{4} + \frac{1}{8} = 1$.

   a. Is J.C. right?

   b. Use diagrams and equations to support your answer.

MY THOUGHTS AND QUESTIONS

MY RESPONSE

Need more room? Use the next page.

Magic Squares

1. Put fractions in the square below so that each row, column and diagonal add to the same amount. A few numbers have been placed to get you started. The total of each row, column and diagonal is equal to $1\frac{2}{3}$.

<table>
<tr><td></td><td>$\dfrac{1}{9}$</td><td>$\dfrac{8}{9}$</td></tr>
<tr><td></td><td>$\dfrac{5}{9}$</td><td></td></tr>
<tr><td></td><td></td><td></td></tr>
</table>

2. Complete the Magic Square below so that each row, column and diagonal add to the same amount. A few numbers have been placed to get you started.

<table>
<tr><td>$\dfrac{7}{8}$</td><td>0</td><td>$\dfrac{5}{8}$</td></tr>
<tr><td></td><td>$\dfrac{1}{2}$</td><td></td></tr>
<tr><td></td><td></td><td></td></tr>
</table>

Magic Triangles 1

Put the following fractions in the circles below so that each side of the Magic Triangle adds to the same Magic Sum. The same six fractions are used in each puzzle and include: $\frac{1}{12}, \frac{1}{6}, \frac{1}{4}, \frac{1}{3}, \frac{1}{2}$ and $\frac{5}{12}$. The sum is written next to the circles.

1. Magic Sum is 1

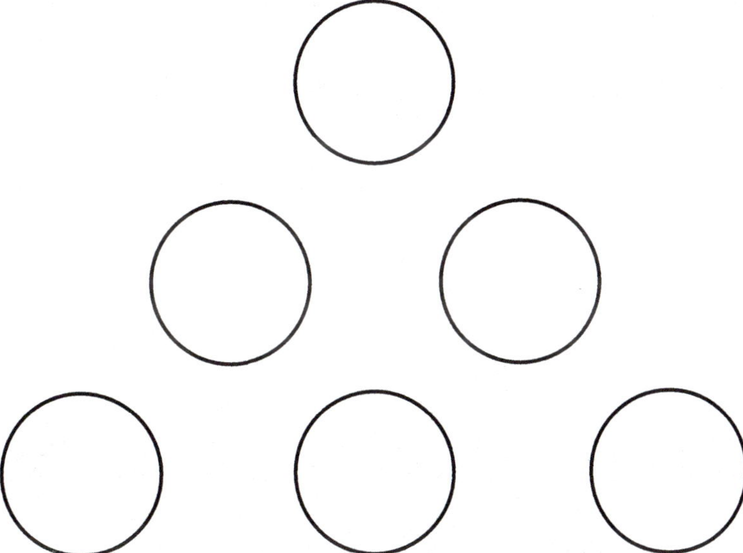

2. Magic Sum is $\frac{3}{4}$

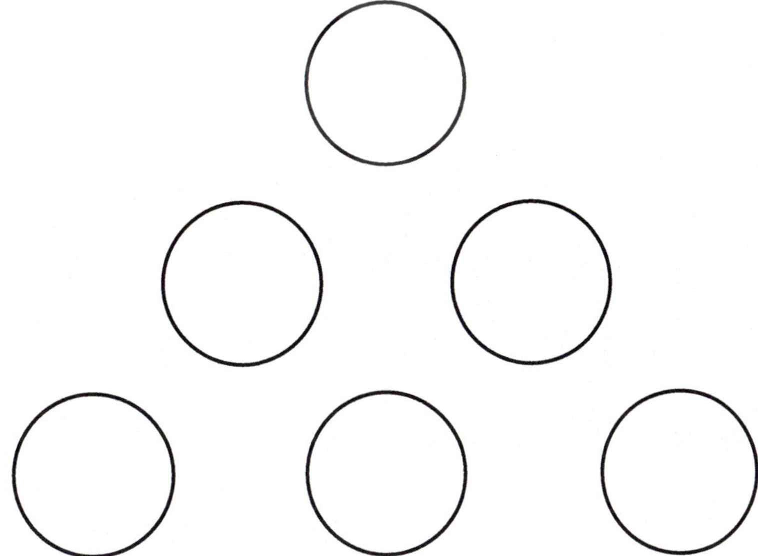

Magic Triangles 2

Put the following fractions in the circles below so that each side of the Magic Triangle adds to the same Magic Sum. The same six numbers are used in each puzzle and include: $\frac{1}{4}, \frac{1}{2}, \frac{3}{4}, 1, 1\frac{1}{4}, 1\frac{1}{2}$.

1. Magic Sum is 3

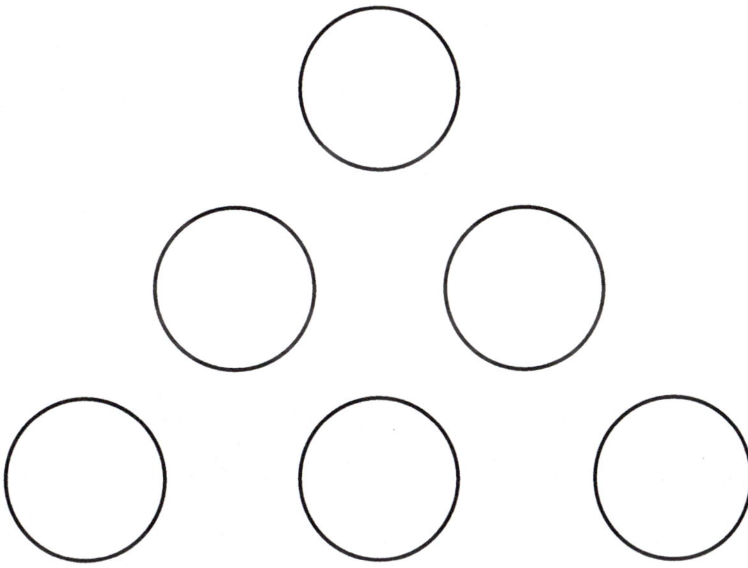

2. Magic Sum is $2\frac{1}{4}$

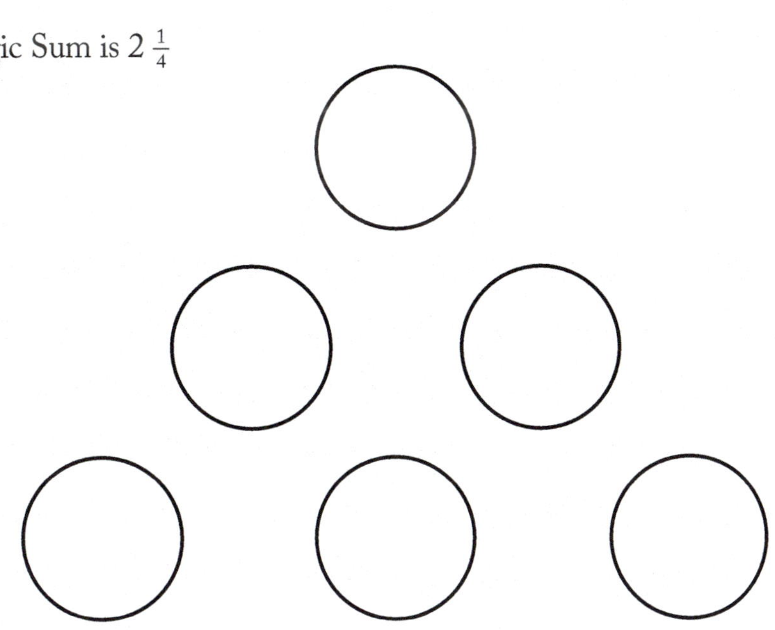

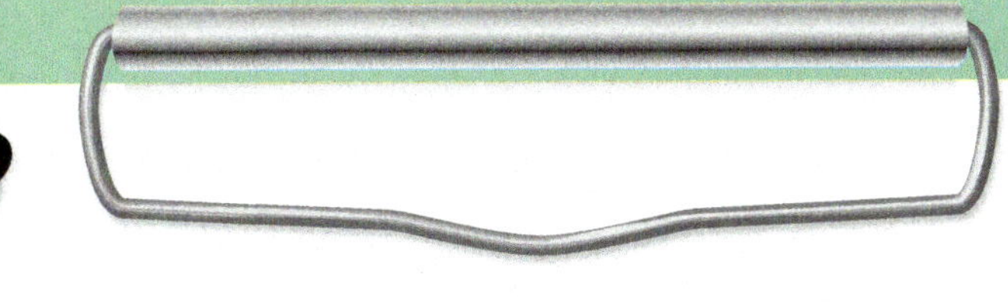

1. This puzzle is a Magic Square where the total of each row, column and diagonal is equal to $1\frac{2}{3}$.

	$\frac{1}{9}$	$\frac{8}{9}$
	$\frac{5}{9}$	
		X

   a. Explain how you would find the value in the box marked with an X. Include any equations and solutions that you use to find this value.

   b. X = _______________

MY THOUGHTS AND QUESTIONS

____

____

MY RESPONSE

____

____

2. a. Using the following fractions, make your own Magic Square with a total of 1 for each row, column and diagonal: $\frac{1}{6}$, $\frac{2}{12}$, $\frac{3}{18}$, $\frac{1}{3}$, $\frac{2}{6}$, $\frac{4}{12}$, $\frac{1}{2}$, $\frac{2}{4}$ and $\frac{3}{6}$.

    b. On the lines below, give a hint to a friend on how to begin.

MY THOUGHTS AND QUESTIONS

MY RESPONSE

Need more room? Use the next page.

Measuring Up

1. Label all the tick marks on the measuring container with the missing fractions and mixed numbers. Be prepared to discuss your reasoning.

2. Abdul has a recipe for punch that calls for $2\frac{1}{2}$ cups of orange juice. Abdul wants to make half a recipe. Write an equation to show how he might solve this.

____

How much orange juice should he use?

____

Mark an A on the diagram of the measuring container to show this amount.

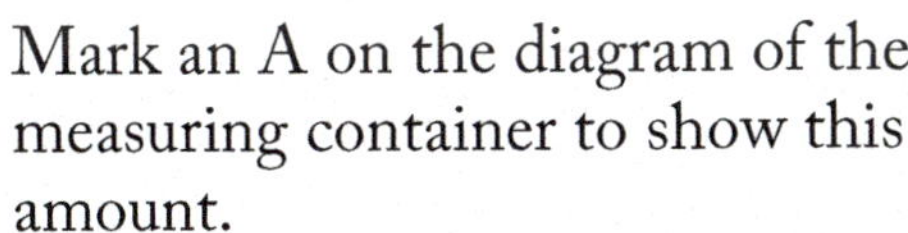
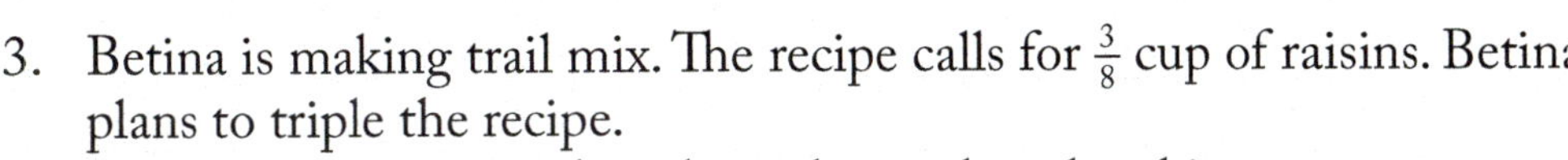

3. Betina is making trail mix. The recipe calls for $\frac{3}{8}$ cup of raisins. Betina plans to triple the recipe.
Write an equation to show how she might solve this.

____

How many cups of raisins should she use?

____

Mark a B on the diagram of the measuring container to show this amount.

3. Charley has a recipe for shortbread that calls for $\frac{2}{3}$ cup of butter. He loves shortbread and plans to make a batch that is $2\frac{1}{2}$ times as large as this recipe. Write an equation to show how he might solve this.

____

How much butter should he use?

____

Mark a C on the diagram of the measuring container to show this amount.

Cooking with Fractions

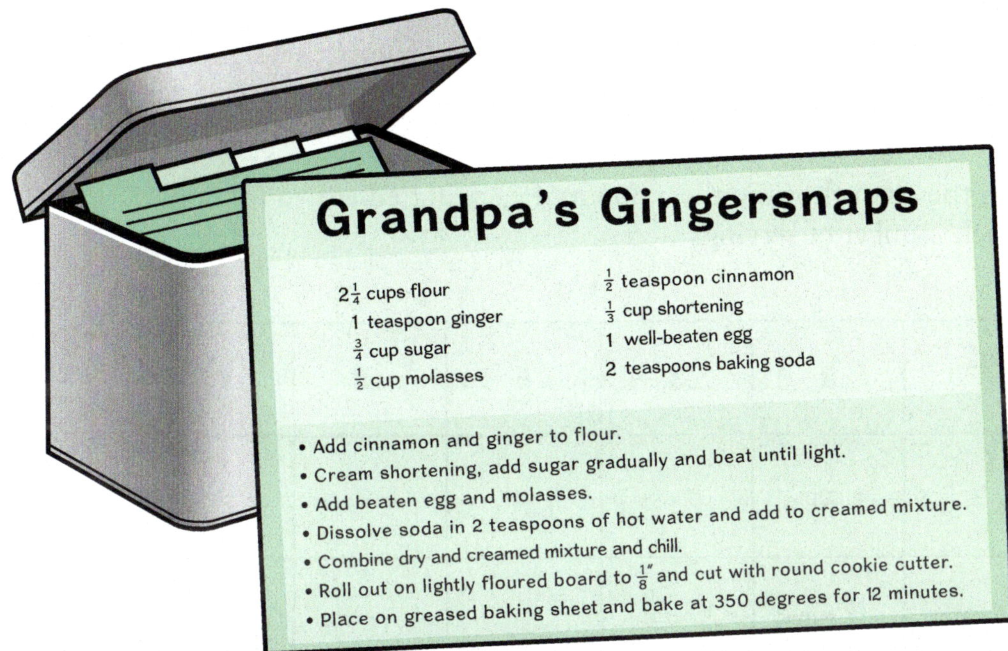

Use Grandpa's recipe for gingersnaps to answer the following.
Be prepared to explain your reasoning.

1. a. Complete the recipe below to show the ingredients you would
       use to triple the recipe.

   _____ cups flour   _____ teaspoon cinnamon

   _____ teaspoons ginger   _____ cups shortening

   _____ cups sugar   _____ eggs

   _____ cups molasses   _____ teaspoons baking soda

   b. On the number line below, show how you might find the amount
      of sugar needed to triple the recipe. Label your number line in
      simplest terms.

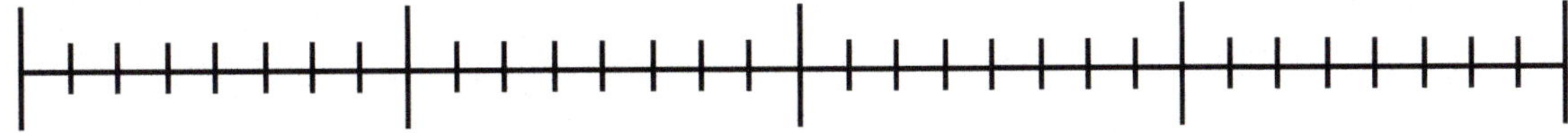

Cooking with Fractions (continued)

c. Write an equation to find the amount of sugar needed to triple the recipe. ____

2. Grandma makes 9 servings of lemonade using 8 cups of water, $1\frac{3}{4}$ cups of sugar and $1\frac{1}{2}$ cups of lemon juice.

a. Complete the chart showing the amount of each ingredient you should use for each number of servings.

Number of Servings	9	3	6	18	24
water	8 cups				
sugar	$1\frac{3}{4}$ cups				
lemon juice	$1\frac{1}{2}$ cups				

b. Explain how you found the amounts of water needed for 24 servings. Use models, equations and words in your explanation.

____

____

____

____

____

____

Student Mathematician: ________________________________ Date: ____________

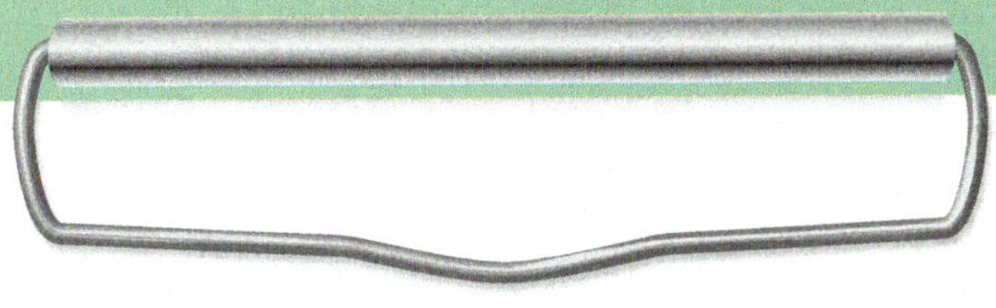

1. Zareen uses the following trail mix recipe:

- 2 cups pretzel sticks
- $\frac{1}{2}$ cup peanuts
- $\frac{3}{4}$ cup banana chips
- $\frac{2}{3}$ cup raisins

a. List the ingredients for $2\frac{1}{2}$ times as much as the original recipe.

____ cups pretzel sticks   ____ cups banana chips

____ cups peanuts   ____ cups raisins

b. Explain how you found the amount of banana chips needed. Include a model, equation and words in your explanation.

Need more room? Use the next page.

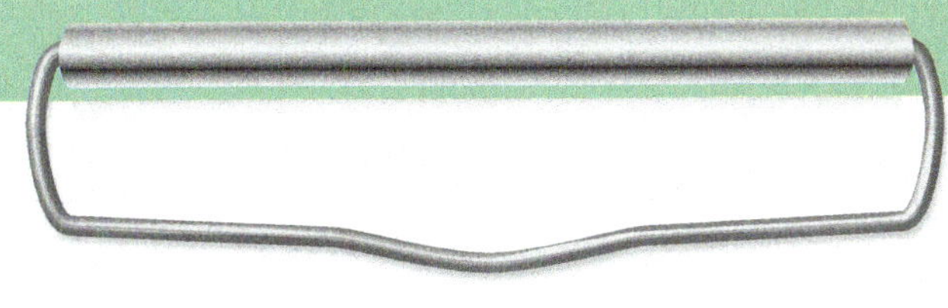

2. Daniel said that he could find the quotient for $\frac{3}{4} \div \frac{1}{2}$ by inverting the $\frac{1}{2}$ and multiplying: $\frac{3}{4} \times \frac{2}{1} = \frac{6}{4} = 1\frac{2}{4} = 1\frac{1}{2}$. Alexa said that she could find the quotient by finding a common denominator and dividing straight across:

$$\frac{3}{4} \div \frac{1}{2} = \frac{3}{4} \div \frac{2}{4} = \frac{3 \div 2}{4 \div 4} = \frac{3 \div 2}{1} = \frac{3}{2} = 1\frac{1}{2}$$

a. Show how you would use Daniel's method to find the quotient for $\frac{2}{3} \div \frac{1}{6}$. ________________________________

b. Show how you would use Alexa's method to find the quotient for $\frac{2}{3} \div \frac{1}{6}$. ________________________________

c. Do you agree with Daniel or Alexa? ______ Explain.

MY THOUGHTS AND QUESTIONS

MY RESPONSE

Need more room? Use the next page.

GLOSSARY

Addends the numbers added together to get a sum, such as the $\frac{1}{2}$ and the $\frac{1}{3}$ in $\frac{1}{2} + \frac{1}{3} = \frac{5}{6}$

Algorithm a method or step-by-step procedure to find an answer that is usually more efficient than other methods

Area model for a fraction a model of the interior region of a two-dimensional space, such as a rectangular array, that represents part of a whole or group by showing the number of equal parts in the whole. For example, the shaded part represents $\frac{6}{8}$, or $\frac{3}{4}$, of the entire rectangle:

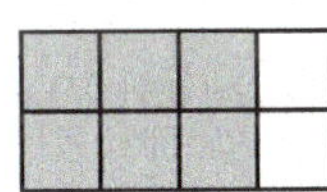

Benchmark a standard against which numbers or other measures can be compared. Numbers like $\frac{1}{2}$ and 1 are often used for comparison to other fractions.

Common denominators denominators in fractions that have the same number of parts, such as the eighths in $\frac{3}{8}$ and $\frac{5}{8}$

Common factors (divisors) numbers that divide evenly into two or more given numbers

Common numerators fractions that have the same numerator, such as $\frac{3}{5}$ and $\frac{3}{4}$

Congruent having exactly the same size and shape

Denominator the number below the line in a fraction, such as the 4 in $\frac{3}{4}$ and $5\frac{1}{4}$. It tells the total amount or size of parts that the numerator counts.

Difference the answer to a subtraction problem, such as the $\frac{1}{6}$ in $\frac{1}{2} - \frac{1}{3} = \frac{1}{6}$

Dividend the quantity in a division problem that is being divided, such as the $\frac{3}{4}$ in $\frac{3}{4} \div \frac{1}{4} = 3$

Divisor the quantity in a division problem by which another quantity is to be divided, such as the $\frac{1}{4}$ in $\frac{3}{4} \div \frac{1}{4} = 3$

Equivalent fractions fractions that have equal value or the same decimal form, such as $\frac{2}{3}$ and $\frac{6}{9}$

Fraction (common fraction) a number that can be written as the quotient of two whole numbers (0 may not be in the denominator). $\frac{a}{b}$ may be thought of as a ÷ b. For example, $\frac{1}{3}$ may be thought of as one whole divided into 3 equal parts or 1 ÷ 3. $\frac{a}{b}$ may be thought of as "a" parts of size $\frac{1}{b}$. Therefore, $\frac{2}{3}$ is 2 parts where each has a size of $\frac{1}{3}$. This also may be 2 wholes divided into 3 equal parts.

Greatest common factor (divisor) the largest number that will divide evenly into two or more given numbers

Identity property of multiplication states that a number multiplied by 1 (including other representations of 1, such as $\frac{3}{3}$) results in a product identical to the given number. For example, $5 \times 1 = 5$, and $1 \times 2 = 2$.

Improper fraction a fraction larger than or equal to 1 whole where the numerator is larger than or equal to the denominator, such as $\frac{8}{5}$ or $\frac{5}{5}$

Least common denominator the smallest number that is a multiple of the denominators of two or more fractions

Least common multiple the smallest common multiple of a set of two or more numbers

Like fractions fractions that have the same denominators, such as $\frac{1}{4}$ and $\frac{3}{4}$

Linear model for a fraction a model, such as a number line or ruler, that represents part of a whole or group by showing the number of equal parts in the whole. For example, the arrow below indicates $1\frac{1}{3}$:

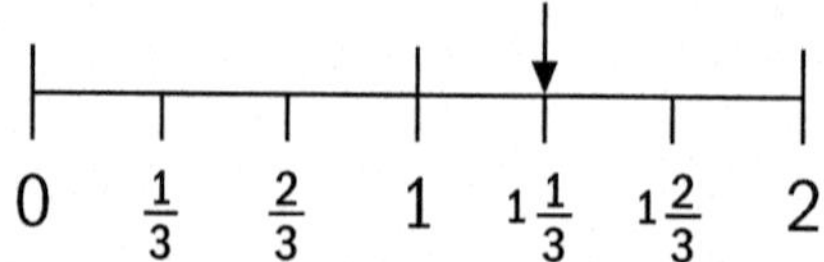

Mixed number a number written as a whole number and a fraction such as $2\frac{1}{2}$

Numerator the number above the line in a fraction, such as the 1 in the fractions $\frac{1}{3}$ and $4\frac{1}{2}$. It tells how many parts of the total, indicated by the denominator, are being counted.

Product the answer to a multiplication problem, such as the $\frac{3}{10}$ in $\frac{3}{5} \times \frac{1}{2} = \frac{3}{10}$

Proper fraction a fraction that is less than 1 whole where the numerator is less than the denominator, such as $\frac{3}{4}$ or $\frac{2}{5}$

Quotient the answer to a division problem, such as the $\frac{3}{5}$ in $\frac{3}{10} \div \frac{1}{2} = \frac{3}{5}$

Relatively prime numbers two or more numbers which share only the number 1 as a common factor, such as 2, 3, and 5

Right hand identity property of division states that a number divided by 1 (including other representations of 1, such as $\frac{3}{3}$) results in a quotient identical to the given number. This element (1) must be to the right of the division sign as in the example $6 \div 1 = 6$. Note that the quotient is not the given number if the element is written to the left of the division sign: $1 \div 6 \neq 6$ (rather, $1 \div 6 = \frac{1}{6}$).

Simplest form (simplify, simplest terms, lowest terms) a way of writing a fraction so there is no whole number other than 1 that will divide evenly into the numerator and the denominator

Sum the answer to an addition problem, such as $\frac{5}{6}$ in the problem $\frac{1}{2} + \frac{1}{3} = \frac{5}{6}$

Unit fraction a fraction with 1 in the numerator and a counting number in the denominator, such as $\frac{1}{8}$

Unlike denominators two or more fractions that have different numbers below the line, such as the 2 and the 3 in the fractions $\frac{1}{2}$ and $\frac{1}{3}$

Unlike fractions fractions that have different denominators, such as $\frac{2}{3}$ and $\frac{3}{4}$

CPSIA information can be obtained
at www.ICGtesting.com
Printed in the USA
LVOW01s1004020816

498488LV00003B/3/P